PRAISE FOR *BEING*

"Because this book is a tapestry of beautiful and authentic self-storytelling, the reader is invited to safely journey inside their own inner terrain. Tremendously helpful!"

PAUL YOUNG, AUTHOR OF *THE SHACK*

"As Karl's story confirms, finding our worth, value and security in the Love that calls us into 'being' actually frees and opens the adventure of 'becoming.'"

PAUL D. FITZGERALD, D.MIN., HEARTCONNEXION SEMINARS

"In a sea of toxic masculinity, *Being* offers another way to engage the spiritual life for men and others. Karl's demonstration of honest vulnerability and change will live deep in your heart as you begin your own journey."

REV. DR. KATY E. VALENTINE, AUTHOR AND PODCASTER

"In telling his sacred story of family dysfunction, personal rejection, fear and anger, and slow progressive healing, Karl Forehand forces us to look within and find our own shadow. And in the process, he reminds us of who we really are in relation to our Source."

REV. DR. MICHAEL J. CHRISTENSEN, PH.D., ACADEMIC DEAN AND PROFESSOR OF THEOLOGY, NORTHWIND INSTITUTE | SEMINARY

"*Being* is not just a book you read, *Being* is a book that reads you."

NORA SOPHIA

"Karl Forehand is offering a vulnerable window into the journey many church people are finding themselves on, after years of being chained to certainty."

ALANA LEVANDOSKI, SONGWRITER, RECORDING ARTIST, PRODUCER, OF POINT VIERGE: THOMAS MERTON'S JOURNEY IN SONG

"*Being* encourages us to look within. A balm for the harried soul, I recommend this book to anyone craving peace but unsure of where to find it."

CHRISTOPHER EAKER, SPIRITUAL DETECTOR, STEPPING STONES LIFE

"There is no way to not hear God in the voice of an authentic word and Karl's here is just that—authentic."

SETH PRICE, HOST OF THE "CAN I SAY THIS AT CHURCH?" PODCAST

"Karl Forehand helps the reader discover our true, eternal being-nature vs. doing-nature, which diminish its unhealthy power over our minds."

ANITA GRACE BROWN, AUTHOR OF *KAMAKAZI YOGI*

"For those like me who have bottomed out on distraction and are ready to go deeper, Karl's journey is a beautiful path into authenticity and wholeness. He's a kind and seasoned guide!"

BRAD JERSAK, AUTHOR OF *A MORE CHRISTLIKE WAY*

"Karl Forehand invites us to journey with him and gives us a bird's eye view of a journey toward wholehearted living and an invitation for the reader to embark on their own path toward self-discovery and wholeness."

MARY JEPPSEN, PH.D.

THE BEING JOURNEY

A 30-Day Companion Guide to
Being: A Journey Toward Presence and Authenticity

Karl Forehand

All rights reserved. No part of this book may be used or reproduced, stored in a retrieval system, or transmitted in any form or by any means, electronic, mechanical, photocopying, recording, scanning, or otherwise, without written permission from the publisher except in the case of brief quotations embodied in critical articles and reviews. Permission for wider usage of this material can be obtained through Shaia-Sophia House by emailing permission@shaiasophiahouse.com.

Copyright © 2021 by Karl J. Forehand.

First Edition

Cover design and layout by Rafael Polendo (polendo.net)
Cover image courtesy of GraphicStock.com

ISBN 978-1-7348234-8-6

This volume is printed on acid free paper and meets ANSI Z39.48 standards.

Printed in the United States of America

Published by Shaia-Sophia House
An imprint of Quoir
San Antonio, Texas, USA

www.ShaiaSophiaHouse.com

To my companion on the Being Journey,
Laura Forehand.

TABLE OF CONTENTS

Introductory Section 8
Introduction and Purpose of this companion guide. 9

Day 1 – Presence and Authenticity. 10
Day 2 – What Do You Feel?. 11

Part I – Don't Waste a Good Crisis. 13
    Day 3 – What is Happening?. 14
    Day 4 – The Weekend 16
    Day 5 – Rejection, Betrayal, Abandonment, Abuse 18
    Day 6 – Going Back to Work 20
    Day 7 – Leaving Home 22
    Day 8 – The Recliner. 24
    Day 9 – Me and My Shadow 26
    Day 10 – Tell Your Story 29

Part II – Going Deeper. 30
    Day 11 – Going Deeper with my Fear. 31
    Day 12 – Going Deeper with Anger 33
    Day 13 – Going Deeper with my Bypassing 35
    Day 14 – Going Deeper with my Voice. 37
    Day 15 – Going Deeper with my Critic. 39

    Day 16 – Going Deeper with my Pain...41

Part III – Learning to Be..43
    Day 17 – Being with Crisis..44
    Day 18 – Being with Poets and Prophets...47
    Day 19 – Being with Community..49
    Day 20 – Being with Nature..52
    Day 21 – Being with Pain..54
    Day 22 – Being with Solitude..56
    Day 23 – Being with Uncertainty..58
    Day 24 – Being with the Divine..60
    Day 25 – Being with the Ignorant..62
    Day 26 – Being with my Dog..64
    Day 27 – Being with my Body..65

Part IV – Moving Forward..67
    Day 28 – Epilogue – Bravery and Vulnerability..................................68
    Day 29 – A Letter to My Future Self..69
    Day 30 – A Letter to the World..71

Focusing Sessions..73
Contact Information..73

INTRODUCTORY SECTION

The Book is divided into sections. You can process this guide in whatever way you desire, but here is a suggestion for each day:

1. Prepare your mind through prayer or mindfulness or whatever clears the distractions and helps you focus. Take your time on all the steps. Do not get in a hurry.

2. Read the chapter of the book indicated in today's reading.

3. Go slowly through the questions and suggestions in today's reading.

4. Contact: The Desert Sanctuary if you have questions or need spiritual direction.

5. As you experience emotions while going through this process, try to have compassion for yourself and your emotions. Instead of shaming yourself, allow yourself to feel the way that you feel.

INTRODUCTION AND PURPOSE OF THIS COMPANION GUIDE.

There are many reasons for reading a book. Sometimes we want to glean information to be used in other areas of our life. Other times, we want to prove a point or gain insight to understand a theory or understand a holy book or to make a case for what we are doing. Books are often educational, entertaining, and captivating. But the purpose of my book called Being is that you the reader would find transformation as you journey through life.

There is a reason it is called a *companion*. As others have said, you are the hero of your story. You are on a journey whether you call it that or not. I hope you are also on an adventure. You have probably realized that this journey is harder than you anticipated. There have been disappointments and setbacks that caused you to doubt yourself and the necessity to the transformational journey you are on.

Because adventures are hard to script, it is helpful to have a *guide* to tell you about what it is going to feel like and how best you can experience this. I wrote the book transparently to show you my journey so that you might gain insight and strength for the road that lies ahead of you.

I would encourage you to take your time processing this guide. Consider each question and suggestion in contemplation before you act. Write freely, then summarize what you are learning. Ask questions and reflect deeply. If you have a mindfulness or prayer practice, incorporate it into the exercises.

I strongly recommend that you seek out spiritual direction one way or another to help you on this 30-day journey. Enlist a counselor or spiritual director to respond when you hit roadblocks you cannot get around. I can help you find someone that understands shadow work and will be a companion for these 30 days. See my contact information in the back of the book.

It is important that you invest this time in completing this heroic journey. It is admirable to consider it, and you will say in the end "It was worth it." I believe in you and will serve as your companion through my story and the questions I pose and possibly through a focusing session or two (see focusing description at the end of this manuscript). There is not a right or wrong answer, only prompts for you to uncover your truth and find your healing.

Be where you are, be who you are, be at peace!

– **Karl Forehand**

DAY 1 – PRESENCE AND AUTHENTICITY

Read the *Introduction* in the book for Day 1 and Day 2

If you have ever attended the typical American church, you have heard the admonition, "Don't just be hearers of the word, but also be doers." It plays well to audiences that enjoy a little guilt with the sermon. When the pastor mentions the signup sheet for the nursery, the attendees barely noticed they have been manipulated and everyone feels better about the world because there is more commitment in the relationship.

Since I was a former pastor, I regret that I used this popular sermon to my advantage, but these days, I am more apt the talk about *being* than doing. If fact, when people ask me for advice or what I think is important, I often say, *"Be where you are and be who you are and then you will be at peace."* I think this is much better advice that just do something.

Take some time to consider these statements.

- What does it mean to be present?

- What does it mean to be authentic?

- Talk about how *doing* has become a trap in your life? What do you gain from it?

DAY 2 – WHAT DO YOU FEEL?

Read the *Introduction* in the book for Day 1 and Day 2

When people are in crisis or come to me for help, instead of asking them what they think, I usually ask them *What do you Feel?* Most of us have stored trauma that I call *shadow material*. We literally store this trauma in our bodies. So, in addition, I might also ask *Where do you feel it?*

Think about the last time you *blew up*. Think about what you felt and where you felt it. As soon as you can, enlist the help of a spiritual director or counselor who understands shadow work and the teaching of Carl Jung. Take the time to find a good companion for this journey. You are just getting started but enlist someone that is impartial and will tell you the truth.

Take some time to consider these statements.

- Think about the last time you *lost it*.

- Talk about the experience.

- Do you have regrets about these times?

- Did it surprise you when it happened?

- Did you feel like you were triggered?

- Were you reacting or responding?

- Are you committed to going deeper, even if it involves some work?

- Take a deep breath and talk about whatever you are feeling right now.

PART I – DON'T WASTE A GOOD CRISIS

This section of the book happened when I went through one of the most difficult weeks of my life. Even though it was difficult, it was one of the most important on my road to recovery. As you go through the days ahead and focus on the different parts of my story, maybe you will want to use it as a tool to examine your story.

I will be your companion as you encounter each obstacle. Be sure to take your time and carefully examine each question and suggestion. As you make discoveries, take time to be with what you discover.

Write everything down, take your time, sit with your discoveries and be at peace.

DAY 3 – WHAT IS HAPPENING?

Read the chapter titled *What is Happening* in the book.

Many of us manage our lives to a fault, never realizing we have issues below the surface that need to be addressed. These issues eventually break out and misbehave. One way to notice whether we have these issues is to observe whether we are reacting or responding to stimuli in our lives.

Just like I was examining my life in the heritage, all of us must take stock of our lives. Often, we long for solutions and answers but forget to examine first what is there. I hope you will take your time with today and every day's questions and truly examine yourself. Take the time to sit with what you find and wrestle with things that seem difficult or impossible to reconcile. There is a path that leads to transformation and I hope you will let my story show you the way.

Take some time to consider these statements.

- Have you ever felt yourself in *full defense mode?* Write down how that felt and what happened.

- Have you ever realized you were taught to ignore pain? In what ways was this manifested in your life?

- Have you ever considered having compassion for the parts of you that feel anger and pain? Describe what you think this would be like and how it could help?

- Have you ever used techniques (especially spiritual ones) to bypass painful realities? Takes some time to sit with this and record your thoughts or observations.

DAY 4 – THE WEEKEND

Read the chapter titled *The Weekend* in the book.

I hope it is not too presumptive to say that my weekend from hell was necessary. I was learning to hear Laura's voice, but I was also learning about my insecurities. There were parts of me that needed healing shouting to be seen and heard. These parts of me needed my compassion and understanding.

When examining our lives, it is important to identify use the phrase, *a part of me feels*. This allows us to identify the stuck places without defining this part as the whole part. In other words, believing that this trauma is driving the car may not be as effective as identifying the part that is stuck and focusing our attention on it without blaming it for everything.

Take some time to consider these statements.

- What are some assumptions you have about situations like this?

- In your life, what would you attribute them to?

- How do you respond to the phrase *a part of me feels……?*

- Take some time to examine that part of you that feels something right now. What is it you are feeling and where do you feel it (shoulders, heart, stomach, etc.)?

- Do not try to understand what you feel. Avoid the urge to say *this probably means* or something similar. Just be with the feeling and have compassion for it.

DAY 5 – REJECTION, BETRAYAL, ABANDONMENT, ABUSE

Read the chapter titled *My History with Rejection* in the book.

There are things in our lives that we try to control. This is usually a response to fear, and it is often like trying to keep a beach ball under water. It works for a while until our arms get tired or we lose focus. Some things we enable to happen. We may not even be aware that we are, but we can often give way to things that do not benefit us. But often things happen to us, we are not prepared to deal with. This is especially true of things that happened to us early in life.

The things that happen to us that we do not deal with (that we were not prepared or equipped for) cause trauma in our bodies. Because we inherently know that these things are detrimental or they produce negative feelings, we stuff them down inside – this is what some call *the shadow*. The shadow is the place where we place things we do not understand or cannot deal with. This produces stuck places in our lives. To heal or shift them, we must bring them out of the dark. This can be a difficult exercise.

Take some time to consider these statements.

- What are your past thoughts about bringing these things out of the dark?

- Do you understand why a younger version of yourself stuffed these emotions down?

- What are some ways that you ignore or subvert these feelings when they come up?

- How could religion play a role in and not be helpful in dealing with shadow?

DAY 6 – GOING BACK TO WORK

Read the chapter titled *Going Back to Work* in the book.

For many of us, routines help us avoid thinking too much about difficult things. Solving other people's problems is often the distraction we need to avoid the problems we have. Sometimes hobbies and other obsessions give us enough *feel good* to get past the nagging suspicion that we have some other *inner work to do*.

I am not suggesting that people are lazy or that they do not want to get better; but we are creatures of survival and we tend use the least number of calories possible to get through our complicated lives. As you consider the following statements, divert some of your valuable and necessary energy to this task for a short time today. I often avoid these types of exercises, but I am finding more and more that they are worth the time.

Take some time to consider these statements.

- In what ways do you use hobbies or work or something else to not think about necessary things? Contemplate and then describe the ways you avoid necessary self-care and repair.

- Have you ever tried to be still for 20 minutes? 10 minutes? 5 minutes? Give it a try—just try to clear your mind 10 minutes. Then try it again tomorrow before you do the next chapter. Record any insights you get from this exercise. Was it hard?

- What is your understanding of contemplative prayer? If you have never heard of it, try to find some basic information about it right now.

- Try just listening in prayer or meditation without any expectations. Record your thoughts here afterward.

DAY 7 – LEAVING HOME

Read the chapter titled *Leaving Home* in the book.

When I was a pastor, I tried to take a sabbatical several times. I always came home early. I got bored because I was just thinking about calendars and future sermons to preach, which was probably good, but it was not the best thing I could be doing. Taking a walk was nice in a different setting, but what do you do the rest of the day, and the next day and so on. What we long for is what Wm. Paul Young describes when he says, *"'Wholeness' is when the way of your being matches the truth of your being."*

To get there we can do what I did in the hermitage. We must go inside. We can do that in a spiritual place or in the back yard. But, in whatever way we find effective, we get away to a place where we will not be distracted or pulled back to the routine of our life. Some of these questions may sound like yesterday, but that is because they deserve a lot of our consideration.

Take some time to consider these statements.

- How comfortable are you with stillness and silence? Discuss whether you think this might improve with practices.

- Do you have any suspicions or preconception about where we find answers? Is it from specific people? Is it a specific place? List all your answers below.

- What are your assumptions about going inside?

DAY 8 – THE RECLINER

Read the chapter titled *It All happened in a Recliner* in the book.

"Our shadow is the place within each of us that contains what we do not know, don't like or deny about ourselves ... Our shadow holds our unattended and not-yet-illuminated conditioning—all the programmed ways we act, think, feel, and choose without knowing why."

– ROBERT AUGUSTUS MASTERS

Take some time to consider these statements.

- What are some things that you do not like about yourself?

- Ask the following questions in stillness:

    - *"What do I feel right now?"* When you know, say *"A part of me feels…"*

    - *"Where do I feel it?"*

- What is it this part of me trying to tell me? Be Patient.

- What things about myself do I tend to deny or gloss over?

DAY 9 – ME AND MY SHADOW

Read the chapter titled *It All happened in a Recliner* in the book.

At this point, it would be a good idea to have a spiritual director or counselor available. Make sure the person is familiar with things like shadow and focusing. Contact: *The Desert Sanctuary* (Karl and Laura Forehand) for recommendations if you need them.

Ensure that you are free from distractions while you do the following exercises. Make plenty of time to sit with what you discover. Marinate in the experience and be patient.

Now that you have identified what you are feeling, check it with and continue to discover what your body is trying to tell you. Take your time, be present. Incorporate some mindfulness if that is already your practice to ensure you are relaxed and present before you begin.

Take some time to consider these statements.

- What do you feel? (Fear, anxiety, anger, pressure, etc.). Say, *"A part of me feels..."*

- Where do you feel it? Say *"A part of me feels …. Here."*

- Be with the feeling. Take your time. Put your hand where you feel this feeling.

- When have you felt this before? Describe what you are feeling now and describe when you have felt this before.

- Go back and try to remember earlier times in your life where you felt this. What was that like? Do you remember the first time you felt it?

- When you find the time in your life you want to focus on, be there with the felt sense that you are feeling it for the first time. Try to show compassion for that earlier version of yourself and spend some time just feeling what they felt.

- You might say to them something like:

    - *"It is no wonder you felt……"*

    - *"I'm here for you, I see you, I hear you…"*

    - *"I've got your back…I will help you…"*

- Stay with them if you need to.

- Sometimes you must speak to your inner critic. Remember to show compassion for them as well. But stay between them and the child.

- Record your thoughts:

  - Try not to say, *"This probably means…"*. Do not analyze, just feel.

  - Write freely, let it out!

- Notice if what you were feeling has shifted or gone way. Talk about that.

- Share with a counselor or spiritual director or The Desert Sanctuary (Karl and Laura Forehand).

DAY 10 – TELL YOUR STORY

Read the chapter titled *Telling My Story* in the book.

It is especially important that we are seen with eyes of grace. So, whether it is a spiritual director or a counselor, please tell your story of your experience yesterday to someone that will show compassion for you and the parts of you involved in this exercise. This is not the time to tell the story to your best friend or your sibling. But telling it to someone who understands the process, is necessary and helpful.

Take some time to consider these statements.

- Journal about you story. What did you experience so far? How do you feel now?

- Why do you think it is important to tell your story?

- What fears will keep you from telling your story?

- Who should you tell your story to? When will you do that?

PART II – GOING DEEPER

When I sat down to write my story about my shadow, my friend Mark Karris assisted me. Among other things, he is a counselor. After I finished part I, he kept telling me to *go deeper*. I really did not want to, but its payed big dividends and I think you will enjoy going on the same journey and using my experience to lead you along this path.

I know that parts of this journey are difficult, but I will be with you through the book and this companion guide. If you need additional help, contact a Spiritual Director or a Counselor, or The Desert Sanctuary (Karl and Laura Forehand) and we will guide you to someone that can help.

DAY 11 – GOING DEEPER WITH MY FEAR

Read the chapter titled *Going Deeper with my Fear* in the book.

Often, we overcome one fear in our lives only to realize we are exposing another. Fear is not necessarily bad. There are times when it is totally appropriate and protects us, but if we continue to let it control us, we may experience deeper problems.

Shame is not an appropriate motivator because it relies on negative programming. When parents tell children not to cry when their bodies sense that it is necessary, it often creates deeper and more problematic issues. Today, we want to see if we can understand our fear a little better.

Take some time to consider these statements.

- Have you ever felt small like Karl described in the book? Explain that experience or experiences.

- What honestly frightens you still? Try to go beyond the surface issues you normally think about. Give it some time.

- Where do you think those fears originate specifically for you? When did you first feel them? What were the circumstances? Avoid general answers like the devil, sin, etc.

- What is one courageous step you could take to overcome that fear or to move away from that fear you identified. Talk about each one you mentioned.

- What obstacles do you see that is keeping you from facing your fears?

DAY 12 – GOING DEEPER WITH ANGER

Read the chapter titled *Going Deeper with Anger* in the book.

Anger is not as simple as it sounds. It is possible that it is often attached to other things like fear. There are times when anger is useful. However, there are also times when it is only the outer symptom of something else.

Take some time to consider these statements.

- Take some time to investigate what might be at the root of your anger?

- When did you last feel it?

- What were the situations that provoked it?

- What emotions did the story about my dad and the wrestling mats bring up?

- Anger, disappointment, rage, compassion, or something else?

- How are the chapters about fear and anger related for you?

- Why do you think little Joey was angry? Can you relate?

DAY 13 – GOING DEEPER WITH MY BYPASSING

Read the chapter titled *Going Deeper with my Bypassing in the book.*

Spiritual bypassing is using spiritual language or making religious excuses for not doing the hard and difficult work of navigating this world we live in. I discovered spiritual bypassing first from a book titled, *Spiritual Bypassing: When Spirituality Disconnects Us from What Really Matters* by Robert Augustus Masters.

In the book I talked about several instances that I have seen spiritual bypassing inadvertently used in religion. This still may be part of your practice, so I hope you can be patient with me and yourself and examine your own practices to see whether they are helping you face the challenges of this life or whether they are using spirituality to help you avoid them.

Take some time to consider these statements.

- What phrases do you use, or have you used in the past to bypass difficult situations?

- How do you experience these phrases in relation to bypassing?
    - I will pray for you or I will keep you in my prayers.

    - God is in control.

    - God has a purpose.

- What is dissociating?

- What has it cost you to bypass situations with catch phrases instead of facing them?

DAY 14 – GOING DEEPER WITH MY VOICE

Read the chapter titled *Going Deeper with my Voice in the book.*

Finding our voice requires us to discover who we are. So many influences keep us from saying what we could say in the places we might say them. As we become more comfortable with who we are, we start to feel the urge to speak our truth. Sometimes, it seems like a complicated maze of obstacles when we begin speaking up for ourselves. People may not understand—we may experience some rejection—but it helps to realize many of the factors that influenced how we got to the place we are.

As we begin to use our voice, it is important to take it slow. We cannot go from being silent to telling people everything we think. And before we speak it may be beneficial to examine how we got to where we are. When we become more whole, our voice will become more centered in who we are. As we become more present and authentic, we will see more clearly when, where and what to say. Our voice will become an asset instead of a liability.

Take some time to consider these statements.

- How has shame played a role in not using your voice? Where did you receive those messages?

- How could sharing out voices help us feel more / less alone and provide tremendous purpose (Mark Karris)?

- What groups, people or images of your past are directing the things you say or ascribe to?

- Talk about the purpose and responsibility of using your voice.

- Knowing who you are: Can you state in one simple statement, "I am a _____, _____, and _____ person. Fill in the blanks with three or four of the most root things that are true about you. For example, my statement says, "I am Karl, I am a playful, adventurous and mystical man!" Take your time.

- Where are some places you can share your voice?

DAY 15 – GOING DEEPER WITH MY CRITIC

Read the chapter titled *Going Deeper with my Critic* in the book.

Our inner critic finds its origins in many places. Often the influential people in our past criticized and shamed us even though they had good intentions. The way we interpreted these messages can have lasting impacts on us. Facing the critic(s) in our life is not to eradicate or remove them in some way. The purpose of confronting the critic, much like our inner child, is to show compassion for them and find healing.

The way I usually approach the critic is simply to ask them to "chill out." In most cases, we can see that the critic was probably trying to protect us, but just used ineffective methods. Part of the issue was how we interpreted the situation at the time. We need to have compassion for all parts of our self—even the critic.

Take some time to consider these statements.

- Who are some of the people that shamed you from your past?

- What are some of the messages the inner critic whispers to you?

- Take some time to focus on each critic and each of the messages you received from them and how you interpreted those messages. What will you do with each of these situations? Will you forgive, show compassion, extend love, or release them in some way. Like other issues of the shadow, your felt sense of their impact may not totally go away, but what can you offer them right now?

- In some extreme cases, you may have to write a letter or make a recording to them. You will not necessarily have to send it, but it may be helpful to produce it. Is there a critic or two that you need to address more directly?

DAY 16 – GOING DEEPER WITH MY PAIN

Read the chapter titled *Going Deeper with my Pain in the book.*

Some amount of pain is common to most of our experiences. When we try to do something new or resolve issues of our past or just get in shape, we notice that the pain often tempts us to give up or try to numb what we feel. The best option is to lean into the pain. In most cases, the pain will subside as we progress through the growing process.

There is no reason to accept abuse from other people, but many worthwhile endeavors cause us to initially feel pain that over time will subside as we get *in shape.*

Take some time to consider these statements.

- What are some things that cause you pain?

- What are your options when you feel pain as you are trying to improve yourself?

- What areas of your life could benefit from you *leaning into the pain?*

- What are some courageous steps you could take and when will you do that?

- What are some practices that will help you endure the necessary pain of growth?

PART III – LEARNING TO BE

Learning to be where we are (presence) and who we are (authenticity) go together. So, even though this section is called *Learning to Be*, understand that it also involves authenticity. It is as much about living authentically (being who we are) as it is about presence (being where we are). As you read through the pages in this section and my story, I hope you will treat it as a guide for your journey. I am finding some peace in my journey and I wish you the same.

DAY 17 – BEING WITH CRISIS

Read the chapter titled *Being with Crisis* in the book.

Some days can seem overwhelming. Because of the current pandemic we are facing, the challenges can seem like too much! We wonder if we can bear all these challenges at once. Is it going to crush us? Are we doomed to fail?

I do not think so.

Times like these require us to especially be present and authentic. These are not easy things, but they are essential. We cannot live in the past or the future, we must be present and understand the situations we are in so that we can recognize opportunities when they come. We also cannot navigate our journey by imitating someone else. Yes, we need guides to show us the way, but we also must be who we are if we are going to have a chance of navigating the path we are on.

It is a crisis, and it is okay to admit that. But we survive with a few simple tools.

Take some time to consider these statements.

- Do you ever try to normalize or minimize serious situations? Describe a few of these.

- Why do we try to plan our adventures? Is this a contradiction?

- Do you ever shame yourself for feeling a certain way? How can you change the things you say in these situations to better serve you?

- What does it mean to be *where you are?*

- What benefits might you realize from being present?

- What does it mean to be *who you are?*

- What benefits might you realize from being authentic

- Describe a couple of courageous steps you could take this week to be more *present* and *authentic?*

DAY 18 – BEING WITH POETS AND PROPHETS

Read the chapter titled *Being with* Poets and Prophets *in the book.*

My theory is that the poets and prophets are trying to tell us about things that are hard to describe. They are experiencing these things and interacting with them, but they generally do not come to a specific conclusion or create a belief system. Most often we are not like that. We want to *wrangle* everything into something specific. The reason the things that poets and prophets say sometimes come true in the future is because what they are wrestling with often contains truth.

We can benefit from the poets and prophets if we experience what they said like a current of understanding instead of a stagnant pool of well-defined knowledge. Poets and prophets are searching and trying to describe the things we long for. They were on a journey like we are to feel and experience true adventure and new discoveries. Let us go on the ride with them!

Take some time to consider these statements.

- Why do you think poets and prophets write and sing and create works they don't fully understand?

- If we search for something deeper, will our conclusions be concrete and definitive, or will it most likely offer more mystery, paradox, and non-dual thinking?

- What happens when we wrangle our discoveries into a belief system?

- Evaluate: Sometimes the things they say come true because what they are discovering contains truth and truth is persistent.

- How is a current of understanding better than a pool of beliefs?

- Listen to Bob Dylan's song *Every Grain of Sand* with the lyrics in front of you. See if this poet's words speak to you. You might even disagree or have points of contention with it. There may be parts of it that deeply resonate with you. Describe the feelings and emotions it evokes in you? What did you gain from it? What does it inspire you to do?

DAY 19 – BEING WITH COMMUNITY

Read the chapter titled *Being with Community* in the book.

For some reason, we associate going to a building and experiencing a show to be the most genuine type of community. But when we talk about our deeper experiences of worship and connection, often that is outside the experience of organized religion. It might be in nature, or in our car, or with family but it is not always within the confines of our acknowledged religious practices. Sometimes, it surprises us when we experience deep connection in places where we did not expect to find it.

My background is Evangelical Christianity and I do not want to disparage its practices or its people; I just hope that we can examine this idea of community honestly. Are we really experiencing true community within the confines of our religious systems or are we just doing what we have always done? I invite you into this thought experiment with me.

Take some time to consider these statements.

- What is your current association with organized religion?

- Can you be vulnerable and experience real connection within the walls of your current religious institution?

- In what ways do you experience true community there or does it fall short? Describe.

- Are there other places you find community?

- What things, that are available within the structure of your religious system, are available outside the organization? For example, sermons, worship music, etc.

- What practices within your experience of organized religion are promoting genuine community?

- Pretend that you never heard of going to your religious facility. What would connection look like in its purest form? Think about this for a while and then write freely.

- Consider what you should add, remove, or modify in your current practices to allow for more genuine community. Consider these guidelines for community:

  - There should be a way for me to *give* in the community

  - There should be a way I can use my voice in the community

  - There should be a way I can gain from the community

DAY 20 – BEING WITH NATURE

Read the chapter titled *Being with Nature in the book.*

Nature not only soothes and enchants us, but it can also be revealing. For however long you meditate on this chapter, make plans to be outside. If you are able, walk barefoot to make the connection to soil below you.

This was a great discovery for me when I found that I have deep connection to nature. I see it differently now. The crickets chirping sound more like music than a distraction. The drumbeat and dance of nature is something not only to observe but to lose myself in.

Take some time to consider these statements.

- Where have you observed the Divine in nature lately?

- In what ways does nature know *where it is* and *what it is*? How are we sometimes different than this?

- If nature does not need approval, what keeps it working?

- Can you relate to the dance and drumbeat of nature? How would you describe it?

- Make plans to simply go out into nature and just be there. Make notes of what you notice.

DAY 21 – BEING WITH PAIN

Read the chapter titled *Being with Pain* in the book.

Many creative options appear when we lean into the pain. Not only do we know for sure how painful it is going to be, but often we get strong or obstacles disappear when we learn against the perceived pain. The sure way to suffer defeat is to quit and numb the pain. These two options almost always end badly.

As you start to lean into pain in your life, I encourage you to take it slowly so as not to injure yourself in another area. Take your time and be reflective and notice how it feels each day.

Take some time to consider these statements.

- What are the three options when things get tough or painful?

- What option is the best and why?

- When should you *quit* in a relationship?

- How can peaceful practices like mindfulness become painful?

- What could you do if you find dark things or uncover things you would rather not deal with when you *go inside?* Develop a plan that includes someone to help you.

DAY 22 – BEING WITH SOLITUDE

Read the chapter titled *Being with Solitude in the book.*

Our first reaction to solitude might be to feel like we are losing in some way. We are usually so busy shuffling schedules and going and doing that when we finally find some quiet at the end of the day, we are exhausted and have several thoughts running through our heads.

Over the last few years, I have had a couple of times where I was unemployed. It was the first times since I was a teenager. But it gave me my solitude when I was rested and ready to receive it. Solitude can be winning because the best of us seems to come forward during these times.

Take some time during this reflection and meditation to truly be in solitude. Admit that this is a good thing, and when you have peace with that, proceed!

Take some time to consider these statements.

- What is your first reaction to solitude?

- What would be some possible benefits from solitude?

- Learn some of the basics of contemplative prayer like *do not expect anything, choose a word to say when you get distracted (like stillness), and just listen for 20 minutes. You may have to work up to this but record your thoughts afterwards.*

- How could you have a "quietness" retreat every day? What would that look like for you?

- When you listen to a meditation today, try being still for 5 minutes.

- Record your thoughts about the poem for this chapter

DAY 23 – BEING WITH UNCERTAINTY

Read the chapter titled *Being with Uncertainty* in the book.

There are many reasons why we like certainty, security, and confirmed assumptions. These things provide us with a temporary peace and make our world smaller and predictive. Our thirst for adventure and mystery and paradox must sit on the bench because we prefer the easy road of certainty about a few things than the uncertainty of much larger endeavors.

Just like when we lean into the pain, I hope you can lean into uncertainty in this exercise.

Take some time to consider these statements.

- Why does uncertainty scare us?

- What other words could we use to describe uncertainty if we chose?

- What really happens when we have a lot of certainty in our lives?

- Is trust most often found in certainty or uncertainty?

- How could we find peace in uncertainty?

- Write down a list of some things you do not know for sure. Circle the ones that you can wait for an answer (you do not have to know right now). Cross through with an "X" the ones that you may never know the answers for. Be still and see if you have any more to add and reflect on this exercise.

DAY 24 – BEING WITH THE DIVINE

Read the chapter titled *Being with the Divine* in the book.

When we see God as something distant that we connect with in certain buildings or around certain people, we minimize where God is and how we can connect with him. Connecting with God does not have to be complicated, but if God is with us and most likely in all things, connecting with the Divine may be much easier than we once thought.

In this exercise, no matter what your beliefs, try to just open to the fact that God is remarkably close. Picture your movement toward God as more of sinking down or resting. As you draw closer try to employ sensations, feelings, emotions, and hearing. Try not to understand God so much as to feel whatever you feel.

Take some time to consider these statements.

- As you are quiet and sensing your emotions, feelings, and sensations, take note of what you are experiencing. Do not analyze it, just record it in one way or another.

- Talk about these feelings, emotions, and sensations?

- Was some of the feelings, emotions, and sensations painful?

- Did this process reveal anything significant to you?

- What are some implications of the idea that God is everywhere?

- What would it change if God were in us?

DAY 25 – BEING WITH THE IGNORANT

Read the chapter titled *Being with the Ignorant* in the book.

I hope this chapter does not sound disparaging. Being with people that have not experienced what we have experienced is often challenging. They do not always understand what we are experiencing and to even examine our new beliefs could possibly threaten them. They are not in any way inferior, but they may not know what we know yet.

Take some time to consider these statements.

- When someone disagrees, is there a way we can accept their opinion without arguing?

- What is cognitive dissonance?

- How would it help to preface everything with "I might be wrong…"?

- How would it be different to lead with our curiosity instead of our anxiety?

- What are some reasons we can be comforted in letting people make their own decisions?

- What is beautiful about telling stories?

DAY 26 – BEING WITH MY DOG

Read the chapter titled *Being with my Dog in the book.*

It always amazes me when I notice what my dog does. He is a pretty great example of authenticity. Like most animals, he always seems to be comfortable with who he is.

Take some time to consider these statements.

- What is it about you that is uniquely you? Take sometime today to refine this list.

- What would change if you lived more authentically? How would your life be better?

- Would you consider your pet a good model of authenticity and/or presence? How?

- In what ways would your life improve if you were more like your pet?

DAY 27 – BEING WITH MY BODY

Read the chapter titled *Being with my Body* in the book.

In the tradition I was raised in, messages about the body were confusing. The body was considered a temple, but also evil, and sometimes a tent to carry the rest of us around. Along the way, we were taught to worry about our bodies, not worry about our bodies, and most of us just emerged confused and embarrassed about most things from the neck down.

Maybe if we pay attention to some modern science, we can redeem this thing called the *body* back into our 21st Century vernacular and discover its important role in healing.

Take some time to consider these statements.

- Have you ever thought that trauma and other such things can be stored in the body?

- What happens eventually when we keep ignoring something that is painful?

- The next time you meditate or pray, take notice slowly of the different parts of your body. What do you notice? Where are you holding tension?

- Consider how you might have thought wrongly about your body?

- What might change if we knew our body held sacred secrets inside.

PART IV – MOVING FORWARD

I hope that you enjoyed the Being Book. In a way it was difficult to write because it required me to be very vulnerable. In another way, it was easy because it is my story, and I did not have invent any characters or imagine a story – I just told mine. I want you to enjoy the book and learn from my journey. I want you feel that you have experienced something beautiful. That makes me happy!

But, better than us both delighting in my experience, I hope you create your own. Let these final chapters be the launching pad for the adventures you are going to create and write and tell others about in your own unique way. Look out over the horizon and ask questions like *What if I am wrong about my current thoughts and belief?* Allow yourself to ponder thoughts like *I wonder what is out there?*

Take the next courageous step, I got your back!

DAY 28 – EPILOGUE – BRAVERY AND VULNERABILITY

Read the chapter titled *Bravery and Vulnerability* in the book.

"Vulnerability sounds like truth & feels like courage. Truth and courage aren't always comfortable, but they are never weakness."

– BRENÉ BROWN

Take some time to consider these statements.

- How do you feel about the possibility that most healing is hard work?

- Use the rest of space provided to:

  ◦ Commit to the work necessary

  ◦ Talk about possible obstacles

  ◦ Talk about how you can be brave

  ◦ Examine why is vulnerability necessary?

DAY 29 – A LETTER TO MY FUTURE SELF

Take some time to consider these statements.

- Write a letter to the future you

- Before you begin, you might want to write a litter to your former self to finish up the shadow work.

- Next, what do you want to say to yourself next year, in five years or 20 years down the road.

- Where will you be? Who will you be? Where are you going to go? What are your intentions?

- What do you hope your future self will do with obstacles?

- How will your future self welcome connection and help?

- How will you be present and authentic?

DAY 30 – A LETTER TO THE WORLD

Take some time to consider these statements.

- Write a letter to the world.

- How are you going to be different?

- What are you going to do?

- What are your intentions?

- Is there someone specific you need to address?

- Is there someone you need to apologize to?

- If you change, what might change in your world?

- Address your family and friends

- Address you detractors

- Address the people that you do not know yet

FOCUSING SESSIONS

Focusing is the tool I most used when dealing with my shadow and learning to be authentic and present. Focusing is a body-oriented process of self-awareness that promotes emotional healing. It involves recognizing how you feel and where you feel it. I can lead you through a simple session in person or online to help you begin to shift your stuck places and help you along in your journey toward wellness.

You body already is trying to speak to you about past trauma and pain. Focusing sessions are similar to a counseling session, but a little more focused and contemplative. Let us lead you through this simple process to help you along in your journey to be where you are and who are

Contact Information:

The Desert Sanctuary

Karl and Laura Forehand

303 W. Opp St.

Rock Port, MO 64482

karl4hand@gmail.com

karlforehand.com

Connect with Karl Forehand

✉ karl@karlforehand.com

🅕 @KarlForehandAuthor

🐦 @karl4hand

Shaia-Sophia House is a collaborative effort of Alexander John Shaia and Nora Sophia's passion to provide a creative home for fresh works from the great traditions. We begin as a publishing house with plans to expand soon into various mediums.

www.ShaiaSophiaHouse.com